The Batsford Book of
STORIES IN VERSE
FOR CHILDREN

TELEPEN

The Batsford Book of

STORIES IN VERSE
FOR CHILDREN

edited by
CHARLES CAUSLEY

illustrated by
CHARLES KEEPING

B. T. BATSFORD LTD · LONDON

First published 1979
Copyright (selection) Charles Causley 1979,
(drawings) Charles Keeping 1979

Set in Plantin 11 on 12 pt.
Printed in Great Britain
by Butler & Tanner Ltd, Frome, Somerset
for the Publishers B.T. Batsford Ltd,
4 Fitzhardinge Street, London W1H 0AH

ISBN 0 7134 1526 6

To Brenda, Gordon, Sarah and Annabelle Morton

CONTENTS

JUSTICE AND INJUSTICE

TALES OF NEAR AND FAR

INTRODUCTION

INTRODUCTION

Even in the age of the atom and of space-travel, the ballad or the story-poem — among the most ancient examples of the art of the poet — still captures the eye and the ear, and sets the imagination alight as strongly as ever. Who, after all, on hearing the opening, bugle-notes of a tale of love or war, of human comedy or tragedy, can resist continuing to its end to see what happens?

The earliest ballads, of course, were sung: but such is the native power and beauty of their texts as handed down to us, that even when divorced from their often haunting tunes they still earn their keep triumphantly as poems in their own right. They also required, within their context of public performance, a degree of instant, though never total, communication: for a true work of art, if it is to be a living organism, must always hold some of its secrets in reserve. Today, we are able to pause and savour the words on the page, brood over their resonances and their half-hidden hints and suggestions. But the invariable simplicity of ballad-language should never deceive us into thinking that the best of such poems lack depth or profundity, or that their authors are without a fundamental seriousness of purpose.

At the same time, we may enjoy and admire the special qualities of the ballad-form: the speed and economy with which a tale is told, the absence of any kind of heavy-handed moralizing. We may respect the plain honesty of the writer who avoids sentimentality, takes no particular side one way or another in a situation of conflict, and who pays us the compliment of allowing the events described to speak for themselves.

Such virtues are also seen to reveal themselves in many of the narrative poems that follow: verse mostly written at periods rather later in time. The tone of voice here is apt to be slightly more relaxed, the story-line — like the delineation of character and place — more involved, detailed and elaborate. Again, a tale in which the emotion and sensibility, as dramatic concepts, act out a drama has always seemed to me as legitimately a narrative piece as one in which a more clearly recognisable physical action moves nearer the surface of a poem.

I have tried, by the addition of a number of street-songs and broadsides, to show something of the very wide range, in manner as well as matter, of a lively and virile form. In all of them, I hope, may be found the life-blood of the true ballad or story-poem: a good tale, memorably told, that in its turn tells us something new of ourselves, each other, and the world—seen and unseen—in which we live.

Whether, in individual cases, the subject is real or imaginary is of secondary importance. 'I love a ballad in print, or a-life', declares the shepherdess Mopsa in Shakespeare's *A Winter's Tale*, 'for then we are sure they are true.' This central allegiance to truth, human sympathy and understanding has always seemed to me to link, in a very real sense, listeners and readers of yesterday, today and tomorrow: for of all poetry, the voice of the ballad is also, unmistakably, the voice of mankind.

CHARLES CAUSLEY
Launceston, Cornwall

CREATURES AND COUNTRYSIDES

THE MAGPIES

When Tom and Elizabeth took the farm
  The bracken made their bed,
And *Quardle oodle ardle wardle doodle*
  The magpies said.

Tom's hand was strong to the plough
  Elizabeth's lips were red,
And *Quardle oodle ardle wardle doodle*
  The magpies said.

Year in year out they worked
  While the pines grew overhead,
And *Quardle oodle ardle wardle doodle*
  The magpies said.

But all the beautiful crops soon went
  To the mortgage-man instead,
And *Quardle oodle ardle wardle doodle*
  The magpies said.

Elizabeth is dead now (it's years ago)
  Old Tom went light in the head;
And *Quardle oodle ardle wardle doodle*
  The magpies said.

The farm's still there. Mortgage corporations
  Couldn't give it away.
And *Quardle oodle ardle wardle doodle*
  The magpies say.

DENIS GLOVER (b. 1912)

THE MULE LADEN WITH CORN, THE MULE LADEN WITH GOLD

Two mules met on a lonely road
Beside a darkening wood
That many a robber had tip-toed through
In search of mulish blood.

One carried gold,
One carried corn,
One was proud of its burden,
The other forlorn.

At the corn-bearing mule the other laughed
As they travelled on down a single path.
'We carry in weight the same heavy load—
But mine is superior, mine is of gold.'

Long after midnight two robbers came.
They ignored the mule that carried the grain.
They fought its companion but fear made it bold,
And it kicked, and refused to give up the gold.

The robbers stabbed the mule in the heart,
And thereby cut its struggle short.
They tip-toed off through the dreadful wood
Loaded with gold and covered in blood.

With its dying breath the mule exclaimed,

'Those who carry their master's gold are fools!
Bray, and tell this to all other mules.
The value of corn is easy to see,
And a world full of gold is useless to me!'

BRIAN PATTEN (b. 1946)

16

THE GOLDEN BOY

In March he was buried
    And nobody cried
Buried in the dirt
    Nobody protested
Where grubs and insects
    That nobody knows
With outer-space faces
    That nobody loves
Can make him their feast
    As if nobody cared.

But the Lord's mother
    Full of her love
Found him underground
    And wrapped him with love
As if he were her baby
    Her own born love
She nursed him with miracles
    And starry love
And he began to live
    And to thrive on her love.

He grew night and day
    And his murderers were glad
He grew like a fire
    And his murderers were happy
He grew lithe and tall
    And his murderers were joyful
He toiled in the fields
    And his murderers cared for him
He grew a gold beard
    And his murderers laughed.

With terrible steel
    They slew him in the furrow
With terrible steel
    They beat his bones from him
With terrible steel
    They ground him to powder
They baked him in ovens
    They sliced him on tables
They ate him they ate him
    They ate him they ate him

Thanking the Lord
Thanking the Wheat
Thanking the Bread
For bringing them Life
Today and Tomorrow
Out of the dirt.

TED HUGHES (b. 1930)

THE DAY BEFORE HARVEST

One day at harvest time the sun
　　Was burning up the sky;
Great Mr. Godlord took a walk
　　Through oats that grew hip high.

He walked bareheaded and unbuttoned
　　Examining every ear,
Wondering just what kind of crop
　　He could expect this year.

And had the ploughing been quite right?
　　Had the sowing been well done?
Was he, great Mr. Godlord worth
　　The praise he always won?

Then in his wide left palm he crushed
　　An ear or two at most,
Studied them closely, gently blew
　　So that no grain was lost.

Davidson came to that same field.
　　'I'll not have these oats spoiled.
This harvest is my blood and sweat.
　　My wife scrimped while I toiled.'

'Yours is it? That's a fine one. Mine!'
　　Old Mr. Godlord spat.
'I ploughed the land, I sowed the seed.
　　Poor man, you must know that.

But if you still insist, my man,
　　I'll tell you what we'll do.
We'll wrestle to find out if it
　　Belongs to me or you.'

They grasped each other then and fought.
   Davidson's skin was torn.
God used his strength. Davidson fell
   Stone dead among the corn.

Such is the usual lot of man.
   Such things are often seen,
Men falling as fat cattle fall
   When clover's thick and green.

Old Mr. Godlord wins and smiles.
   'Brother, you must have known
These crops were mine and always will
   Be mine and mine alone?

Then in his wide left palm he crushes
   An ear or two at most,
Studies them closely, gently blows
   So that no grain is lost.

JAN KASPROWICZ (1860-1926)

translated from the Polish by
Jerzy Peterkiewicz and Burns Singer

THE AMERICAN TRAVELLER

To Lake Aghmoogenegamook,
    All in the State of Maine,
A Man from Wittequergaugaum came
    One evening in the rain.

'I am a traveller,' said he,
    'Just started on a tour,
And go to Nomjamskillicock
    Tomorrow morn at four.'

He took a tavern bed that night;
    And, with the morrow's sun,
By way of Sekledobskus went,
    With carpet-bag and gun.

A week passed on; and next we find
    Our native tourist come
To that sequestered village called
    Genasagarnagum.

From thence he went to Absequoit,
    And there, quite tired of Maine —
He sought the mountains of Vermont,
    Upon a railroad train.

Dog Hollow, in the Green Mount State,
    Was his first stopping place;
And then Skunk's Misery displayed
    Its sweetness and its grace.

By easy stages then he went
    To visit Devil's Den;
And Scramble Hollow, by the way,
    Did come within his ken.

Then *via* Nine Holes and Goose Green
   He travelled through the State;
And to Virginia, finally,
   Was guided by his fate.

Within the Old Dominion's bounds
   He wandered up and down;
Today, at Buzzard Roost ensconced,
   Tomorrow at Hell Town.

At Pole Cat, too, he spent a week,
   Till friends from Bull Ring came,
And made him spend a day with them
   In hunting forest-game.

Then, with his carpet bag in hand,
   To Dog Town next he went,
Though stopping at Free Negro Town,
   Where half a day he spent.

From thence, to Negationburg
   His route of travel lay;
Which having gained, he left the State
   And took a southward way.

North Carolina's friendly soil
   He trod at fall of night,
And, on a bed of softest down,
   He slept at Hell's Delight.

Morn found him on the road again,
   To Lousy Level bound;
At Bull's Tail, and Lick Lizard, too,
   Good provender he found.

The country all about Pinch Gut
   So beautiful did seem
That the beholder thought it like
   A picture in a dream.

But the plantations near Burnt Coat
  Were even finer still,
And made the wondering tourist feel
  A soft delicious thrill.

At Tear Shirt, too, the scenery
  Most charming did appear,
With Snatch It in the distance far,
  And Purgatory near.

But, spite of all these pleasant scenes,
  The tourist stoutly swore
That home is brightest, after all,
  And travel is a bore.

So back he went to Maine straightway:
  A little wife he took;
And now is making nutmegs at
  Moosehicmagunticook.

ROBERT H. NEWELL (1836-1901)

MAD JACK'S COCKATOO

There's a man that went out in the floodtime and drought,
  By the banks of the outer Barcoo,
And they called him Mad Jack 'cause the swag on his back
  Was the perch for an old cockatoo.

By the towns near and far, in sheds, shanty and bar
  Came the yarns of Mad Jack and his bird,
And this tale I relate (it was told by a mate)
  Is just one of the many I've heard.

Now Jack was a bloke who could drink, holy smoke,
  He could swig twenty mugs to my ten,
And that old cockatoo, it could sink quite a few,
  And it drank with the rest of the men.

One day when the heat was a thing hard to beat,
  Mad Jack and his old cockatoo
Came in from the West — at the old Swagman's Rest
  Jack ordered the schooners for two.

And when these had gone down he forked out half a crown,
  And they drank till the money was spent:
Then Jack pulled out a note from his old tattered coat
  And between them they drank every cent.

Then the old cockatoo, it swore red, black and blue,
  And it knocked all the mugs off the bar;
Then it flew through the air, and it pulled at the hair
  Of a bloke who was drinking Three Star.

And it jerked out the pegs from the barrels and kegs,
  Knocked the bottles all down from the shelf,
With a sound like a cheer it dived into the beer,
  And it finished up drowning itself.

When at last Mad Jack woke from his sleep he ne'er spoke,
  But he cried like a lost husband's wife,
And each quick falling tear made a flood with the beer,
  And the men had to swim for their life.

Then Mad Jack he did drown; when the waters went down
  He was lying there stiffened and blue,
And it's told far and wide that stretched out by his side
  Was his track-mate — the old cockatoo.

ANONYMOUS

Barcoo: a watercourse in Queensland, Australia
swag: bundle of personal belongings
schooner: large-sized beer glass

THE BURIAL

Will's ferret was buried this morn:
    When Samuel came down from his bed,
He whisper'd, with aspect forlorn,
    'O Kitty, Will's ferret is dead.'

And Kitty soon told it to Mark,
    And Mark to the rest of his clan.
We sorrow'd with visages dark,
    As if we were mourning a man.

'Come, Ann, let us lay her to rest,
    And you must prepare us a bier:
We will heap the cold earth on her breast;'
    And we wiped from our eyelids a tear.

So Ann made a coffin so small,
    Of cast-off brown paper and thread:
This served for a shroud and a pall—
    False trappings, unknown to the dead.

And Samuel was sexton and clerk,
    And Benjamin bearer so brave,
While Kitty, and Jacob, and Mark,
    Soon bore her away to the grave.

My mother was curious enow,
    And so she came softly behind,
Well pleased with her children, I trow,
    Who to the poor brute were so kind.

'Neath the hawthorn its grave was dug deep,
    With sharp-pointed pickaxe and spade.
Lie down, little ferret, and sleep
    On the couch that affection has made.

JOHN HARRIS (1820-84)
    John Harris was a Cornish tin and copper miner
    who worked underground for over twenty years.

ORIGIN OF FIRE

In the old days men ate raw flesh
And had no knowledge of fire.
Also they had no weapons
And hunted the game with their bare hands.

A boy went hunting one day with his brother-in-law.
They saw a macaw's nest up perched on a cliff-ledge.
They built a ladder and the boy climbed up to the ledge.
In the nest were two eggs.
The boy took them and threw them down to his
    brother-in-law
But in the air they turned into jagged stones
Which as he went to catch them cut his hands.
He was very angry.
He thought the boy was trying to kill him.
He took the ladder down broke it and went away.

The boy was on the ledge for many days and nights
Dying slowly of hunger
Eating his own excrement
Until one day the jaguar passed by
With his bow and arrows

And seeing a shadow cast ahead of him on the ground
Looked up and saw the boy.
The jaguar mended the ladder helped the boy down
Took him back to his home and revived him
Feeding him cooked meat.

The jaguar loved the boy and treated him as his son
Calling him the foundling
But the jaguar's wife was very jealous of him
And when the jaguar was away she never missed a chance
To scratch him or to knock him over.

The boy complained to the jaguar that he was always
    frightened
So the jaguar gave him a bow and arrow
And taught him how to use them.
The next time the jaguar's wife attacked him
He shot an arrow at her and killed her.

The boy was terrified by what he had done.
He took his bow and a large piece of cooked meat
And escaped into the jungle.
After many days wandering he reached his own village
And told his people all the things that had happened to
    him
Showing them the meat and the bow.
The men were very excited by his discoveries
And they set off on an expedition to the jaguar's home
To steal his weapons
And to steal his fire.

What you take from people
They will never find again.
Now the jaguar has no weapons
Except his hatred for man.
He eats no cooked meat
But swallows the raw flesh of his victims.
And only the reflection and the memory of fire
Burn in his eyes.

CHRISTOPHER HAMPTON (b. 1946)

from the play Savages

THE HOLY WELL

As it fell out one May morning,
    And upon one bright holiday,
Sweet Jesus asked of his dear mother,
    If he might go to play.

'To play, to play, sweet Jesus shall go,
    And to play pray get you gone;
And let me hear of no complaint
    At night when you come home.'

Sweet Jesus went down to yonder town,
    As far as the Holy Well,
And there did see as fine children
    As any tongue can tell.

He said, 'God bless you every one,
    And your bodies Christ save and see:
Little children, shall I play with you,
    And you shall play with me?'

But they made answer to him, 'No:
    They were lords and ladies all;
And he was but a maiden's child,
    Born in an ox's stall.'

Sweet Jesus turnèd him around,
    And he neither laughed nor smiled,
But the tears came trickling from his eyes
    To be but a maiden's child.

Sweet Jesus turnèd him about,
    To his mother's dear home went he,
And said, 'I have been in yonder town,
    As far as you can see.

'I have been down in yonder town
    As far as the Holy Well,
There did I meet as fine children
    As any tongue can tell.

'I bid God bless them every one,
    And their bodies Christ save and see:
Little children, shall I play with you,
    And you shall play with me?

'But they made answer to me, No:
    They were lords and ladies all;
And I was but a maiden's child,
    Born in an ox's stall.' –

'Though you are but a maiden's child,
    Born in an ox's stall,
Thou art the Christ, the King of heaven,
    And the Saviour of them all.

'Sweet Jesus, go down to yonder town
    As far as the Holy Well,
And take away those sinful souls,
    And dip them deep in hell.'

'Nay, nay,' sweet Jesus said,
    'Nay, nay, that may not be;
For there are too many sinful souls,
    Crying out for the help of me.'

ANONYMOUS

ENDS AND BEGINNINGS

HERE WE GO ROUND THE ROUND HOUSE

The Round House, c.1830, is
built over a broken market cross at
Newport, Launceston, in Cornwall.

Here we go round the Round House
In the month of one,
Looking to the eastward
For the springing sun.
The sky is made of ashes,
The trees are made of bone,
And all the water in the well
Is stubborn as a stone.

Here we go round the Round House
In the month of two
Waiting for the weather
To thaw my dancing shoe.
In St Thomas River
Hide the freckled trout,
But for dinner on Friday
I shall pull one out.

Here we go round the Round House
In the month of three,
Listening for the bumble
Of the humble-bee.
The light is growing longer,
The geese begin to lay,
The song-thrush in the church-yard
Charms the cold away.

Here we go round the Round House
In the month of four,
Watching a couple dressed in green
Dancing through the door.

One wears a wreath of myrtle,
Another, buds of thorn:
God grant that all men's children
Be as sweetly born.

Here we go round the Round House
In the month of five,
Waiting for the summer
To tell us we're alive.
All round the country
The warm seas flow,
The devil's on an ice-cap
Melting with the snow.

Here we go round the Round House
In the month of six;
High in the tower
The town clock ticks.
Hear the black quarter-jacks
Beat the noon bell;
They say the day is half away
And the year as well.

Here we go round the Round House
In the month of seven,
The river running thirsty
From Cornwall to Devon.
The sun is on the hedgerow
The cattle in the stream,
And one will give us strawberries
And one will give us cream.

Here we go round the Round House
In the month of eight
Hoping that for harvest
We shall never wait.
Slyly the sunshine
Butters up the bread
To bear us through the winter
When the light is dead.

Here we go round the Round House
In the month of nine,
Watching the orchard apple
Turning into wine.
The day after tomorrow
I'll take one from the tree
And pray the worm will do no harm
If it comes close to me.

Here we go round the Round House
In the month of ten
While the cattle winter
In the farmer's pen.
Thick the leaves are lying
On the coppice floor;
Such a coat against the cold
Never a body wore.

Here we go round the Round House
In the month of eleven,
The sea-birds swiftly flying
To the coast of heaven.
The plough is in the furrow,
The boat is on the strand;
May I be fed on fish and bread
While water lies on land.

Here we go round the Round House
In the month of twelve,
The hedgers break the brier
And the ditchers delve.
As we go round the Round House
May the moon and sun
Guide us to tomorrow
And the month of one:
And life be never done.

CHARLES CAUSLEY (b. 1917)

A Bush Christening

On the outer Barcoo where the churches are few,
   And men of religion are scanty,
On a road never cross'd 'cept by folk that are lost
   One Michael Magee had a shanty.

Now this Mike was the dad of a ten-year-old lad,
   Plump, healthy, and stoutly conditioned;
He was strong as the best, but poor Mike had no rest
   For the youngster had never been christened.

And his wife used to cry, 'If the darlin' should die
   Saint Peter would not recognize him.'
But by luck he survived till a preacher arrived,
   Who agreed straightaway to baptize him.

Now the artful young rogue, while they held their collogue,
   With his ear to the keyhole was listenin';
And he muttered in fright, while his features turned white,
   'What the divil and all is this christenin'?'

He was none of your dolts — he had seen them brand colts,
   And it seemed to his small understanding,
If the man in the frock made him one of the flock,
   It must mean something very like branding.

So away with a rush he set off for the bush,
   While the tears in his eyelids they glistened —
''Tis outrageous', says he, 'to brand youngsters like me;
   I'll be dashed if I'll stop to be christened!'

Like a young native dog he ran into a log,
   And his father with language uncivil,
Never heeding the 'praste', cried aloud in his haste
   'Come out and be christened, you divil!'

But he lay there as snug as a bug in a rug,
And his parents in vain might reprove him,
Till His Reverence spoke (he was fond of a joke),
'I've a notion,' says he, 'that'll move him.

'Poke a stick up the log, give the spalpeen a prog;
Poke him aisy — don't hurt him or maim him;
'Tis not long that he'll stand, I've the water at hand,
As he rushes out this end I'll name him.

'Here he comes, and for shame ye've forgotten the name —
Is it Patsy or Michael or Dinnis?'
Here the youngster ran out, and the priest gave a shout —
'Take your chance, anyhow, wid "Maginnis"!'

As the howling young cub ran away to the scrub
Where he knew that pursuit would be risky,
The priest, as he fled, flung a flask at his head
That was labelled 'Maginnis's Whisky!'

Now Maginnis Magee has been made a J.P.,
And the one thing he hates more than sin is
To be asked by the folk, who have heard of the joke,
How he came to be christened Maginnis!

A. B. ('BANJO') PATERSON (1864-1941)

As I was going down Treak Street

As I was going down Treak Street
For half a pound of treacle,
Who should I meet but my old friend Micky Thumps.
He said to me, 'Wilt thou come to our wake?'
I thought a bit,
I thought a bit,
I said I didn't mind:
So I went.

As I was sitting on our doorstep
Who should come by but my old friend Micky Thumps'
    brother.
He said to me, 'Wilt thou come to our house?
Micky is ill.'
I thought a bit,
I thought a bit,
I said I didn't mind:
So I went.

And he were ill:
He were gradely ill.
He said to me,
'Wilt thou come to my funeral, mon, if I die?'
I thought a bit,
I thought a bit,
I said I didn't mind:
So I went.

And it *were* a funeral.
Some stamped on his grave:
Some spat on his grave:
But I scraped my eyes out for my old friend Micky Thumps.

ANONYMOUS

wake: a holiday party
gradely: really; properly

42

In Memoriam

Willie had a purple monkey climbing on a yellow
    stick,
And when he had sucked the paint all off it made him
    deadly sick;
And in his latest hours he clasped that monkey in his
    hand,
And bade good-bye to earth and went into a better
    land.

Oh no more he'll shoot his sister with his little wooden
    gun;
And no more he'll twist the pussy's tail and make her
    yowl for fun.
The Pussy's tail now stands out straight; the gun is
    laid aside;
The monkey doesn't jump around since little Willie
    died.

MAX ADELER (1841-1915) (pen-name of C. H. Clark)

Dunkley's Dewpond

A child fell in Dunkley's dewpond.
It was Spring and the pond
Held six hundred gallons of dew,
And the child began to drown in the depths of dew
That it thought were shallows

Till Dunkley arrived from the Down
Driving acres of sheep
All asleep in a trance of snow
And a voice gargled, 'Help!'

Dunkley heard what he thought was a voice
What he thought was gargling
What he thought was *help*
And he had good ears
So wasted no time:

He took off his hat
To reveal pink bone,
And calling "Old on!", hung his hat on a twig
And stepped from his wellington boots,
Pulled his heels and his ankles
Out of socks without a toe,
Hung his socks on another twig
Then danced up and down in an agony of nettles.

The child came up once again
Spitting out tadpoles,
And Dunkley said, dropping trousers with his
    aitches,
"Old on!' And the child went down
While the tadpoles grew imperceptibly into frogs
And Dunkley cast several clouts
And hung them on twigs, including an overcoat
With pockets full of lambs
Calling *Baa!* till his white woollen vest
Walked away across the grass
And nibbled at the clover with some sheep.

There were bubbles in the pond
And the bubbles held the echo of a voice
As Dunkley with his braces on a willow
Put himself this problem:
Laden with a six-stone child
Why was the level of the pond
Unrisen? "Old on!' he called
And pondered till he thought he saw the answer:
The child was in the pond
But the pond was in the child,
About six stone jars of the pond,
So they cancelled out, and the bubbles stopped
    blowing.

Picture Dunkley now, nude before a flock of sheep
And a pocketful of lambs saying *Baa!*
With his pink skull, his sharp elbows
And his shepherd's crotch, looking
At the newly pregnant water:
Did he hesitate? At once
He immersed first his twin slim ankles
Then his blue-veined calves, polished kneecaps,
    nerves,
Till clenching his thighs
He stepped to his distraction in the still wet centre.

Not a bubble stirred. Dunkley with his fingers up
    his nose
Went down into the ooze and the bubbles stirred
And the ooze oozed, but he didn't find a thing,
Not the hank of a hair nor a little cotton sock
Or that's his story. But Dunkley's daft
Or that's his story, and he's told it
Several times. He came out slowly,
His eyeballs raw as vetches
And his kneecaps full of water,
And regained the painful shore.

Yes: his sheep *were* there,
His clothes were *there*
But *where* was the child?

And who was there missing who weighed six stones
And was given to water?
He went to the village but no-one could tell,
To the town across the hill
But no-one could care.
He's walked round asking for many a year.

If any such there be
Then his mammy's done weeping
And his daddy's done weeping
And the sky's done weeping

But the dewpond is full
With the necessary tears.

MICHAEL BALDWIN (b. 1930)

GOLIATH AND DAVID

(For D. C. T., killed at Fricourt, March 1916)

Once an earlier David took
Smooth pebbles from the brook:
Out between the lines he went
To that one-sided tournament,
A shepherd boy who stood out fine
And young to fight a Philistine
Clad all in brazen mail. He swears
That he's killed lions, he's killed bears,
And those that scorn the God of Zion
Shall perish so like bear or lion.
But...the historian of that fight
Had not the heart to tell it right.

Striding within javelin range
Goliath marvels at this strange
Goodly raced boy so proud of strength.
David's clear eye measures the length;
With hand thrust back, he cramps one knee,
Poises a moment thoughtfully,
And hurls with a long vengeful swing.
The pebble, humming from the sling
Like a wild bee, flies a sure line
For the forehead of the Philistine;
Then...but there comes a brazen clink,
And quicker than a man can think
Goliath's shield parries each cast.
Clang! clang! and clang! was David's last.
Scorn blazes in the Giant's eye,
Towering unhurt six cubits high.
Says foolish David, 'Damn your shield!
And damn my sling! but I'll not yield.'
He takes his staff of Mamre oak,
A knotted shepherd-staff that's broke
The skull of many a wolf and fox
Come filching lambs from Jesse's flocks.
Loud laughs Goliath, and that laugh

Can scatter chariots like blown chaff
To rout: but David, calm and brave,
Holds his ground, for God will save.
Steel crosses wood, a flash, and oh!
Shame for beauty's overthrow!
(God's eyes are dim, his ears are shut.)
One cruel backhand sabre cut —
'I'm hit! I'm killed!' young David cries,
Throws blindly forward, chokes...and dies.

And look, spike-helmeted, grey, grim,
Goliath straddles over him.

ROBERT GRAVES (b. 1895)

Mamre: Abraham, the founder of the Hebrew
nation, once camped beneath the oak trees of
Mamre, a plain near the city of Hebron in Israel.
See *Genesis,* Chapter 13, v. 18.

The Bible story of David and Goliath is told in
the *1st Book of Samuel,* Chapter 17.

While serving as a Captain in the Royal Welch
Fusiliers Robert Graves was himself wounded
in the Battle of the Somme in 1916, and
reported missing. In his autobiography of
those days, *Goodbye to All That,* first
published in 1929, he tells us that many
volunteers had falsified their ages in order to
join up. One man in his platoon, for instance,
was sixty-three; another, a collier, had given his
age as eighteen, but was really only fifteen.

THE EXPLOSION

On the day of the explosion
Shadows pointed towards the pithead:
In the sun the slagheap slept.

Down the lane came men in pitboots
Coughing oath-edged talk and pipe-smoke,
Shouldering off the freshened silence.

One chased after rabbits; lost them;
Came back with a nest of lark's eggs;
Showed them; lodged them in the grasses.

So they passed in beards and moleskins,
Fathers, brothers, nicknames, laughter,
Through the tall gates standing open.

At noon, there came a tremor; cows
Stopped chewing for a second; sun,
Scarfed as in a heat-haze, dimmed.

The dead go on before us, they
Are sitting in God's house in comfort,
We shall see them face to face —

Plain as lettering in the chapels
It was said, and for a second
Wives saw men of the explosion

Larger than in life they managed —
Gold as on a coin, or walking
Somehow from the sun towards them,

One showing the eggs unbroken.

PHILIP LARKIN (b. 1922)

THE BALLAD OF
MOLL MAGEE

Come round me, little childer;
There, don't fling stones at me
Because I mutter as I go;
But pity Moll Magee.

My man was a poor fisher
With shore lines in the say;
My work was saltin' herrings
The whole of the long day.

And sometimes from the saltin' shed
I scarce could drag my feet,
Under the blessed moonlight,
Along the pebbly street.

I'd always been but weakly,
And my baby was just born;
A neighbour minded her by day,
I minded her till morn.

I lay upon my baby;
Ye little childer dear,
I looked on my cold baby
When the morn grew frosty and clear.

A weary woman sleeps so hard!
My man grew red and pale,
And gave me money, and bade me go
To my own place, Kinsale.

He drove me out and shut the door,
And gave his curse to me;
I went away in silence,
No neighbour could I see.

The windows and the doors were shut,
One star shone faint and green,
The little straws were turnin' round
Across the bare boreen.

I went away in silence:
Beyond old Martin's byre
I saw a kindly neighbour
Blowin' her mornin' fire.

She drew from me my story —
My money's all used up,
And still, with pityin', scornin' eye,
She gives me bite and sup.

She says my man will surely come
And fetch me home agin;
But always, as I'm movin' round,
Without doors or within,

Pilin' the wood or pilin' the turf,
Or goin' to the well,
I'm thinkin' of my baby
And keenin' to mysel'.

And sometimes I am sure she knows
When, openin' wide His door,
God lights the stars, His candles,
And looks upon the poor.

So now, ye little childer,
Ye won't fling stones at me;
But gather with your shinin' looks
And pity Moll Magee.

W. B. YEATS (1865-1939)

boreen: lane
keenin': wailing cry or song lamenting the dead

The Wreck of
the 'Julie Plante'

A Legend of Lac St Pierre

On wan dark night on Lac St Pierre,
  De win' she blow, blow, blow,
An' de crew of de wood scow 'Julie Plante'
  Got scar't an' run below –
For de win' she blow lak hurricane
  Bimeby she blow some more,
An' de scow bus' up on Lac St Pierre
  Wan arpent from de shore.

De captinne walk on de fronte deck,
  An' walk de hin' deck too –
He call de crew from up de hole
  He call de cook also.
De cook she's name was Rosie,
  She come from Montreal,
Was chambre maid on lumber barge,
  On de Grande Lachine Canal.

De win' she blow from nor'-eas'-wes', –
  De sout' win' she blow too,
W'en Rosie cry 'Mon cher captinne,
  Mon cher, w'at I shall do?'
Den de Captinne t'row de big ankerre,
  But still de scow she dreef,
De crew he can't pass on de shore,
  Becos' he los' hees skeef.

De night was dark lak' wan black cat,
  De wave run high an' fas',
W'en de captinne tak' de Rosie girl
  An' tie her to de mas'.
Den he also tak' de life preserve,
  An' jomp off on de lak',
An' say, 'Good-bye, ma Rosie dear,
  I go drown for your sak'.'

Nex' morning very early
    'Bout ha'f-pas' two — t'ree — four —
De captinne — scow — an' de poor Rosie
    Was corpses on de shore,
For de win' she blow lak' hurricane
    Bimeby she blow some more,
An' de scow bus' up on Lac St Pierre,
    Wan arpent from de shore.

MORAL

Now all good wood scow sailor man
    Tak' warning by dat storm
An' go an' marry some nice French girl
    An' leev on wan beeg farm.
De win' can blow lak' hurricane
    An' s'pose she blow some more,
You can't get drown on Lac St Pierre
    So long you stay on shore.

WILLIAM HENRY DRUMMOND (1854-1907)

arpent: a measure of about an acre of land

LOVE LOST AND WON

ROGER AND DOLLY

Young Roger came tapping at Dolly's window,
 Tumpaty, tumpaty, tump.
He begg'd for admittance, she answer'd him, No!
 Glumpaty, glumpaty, glump.
My Dolly, my dear, your true love is here,
 Dumpaty, dumpaty, dump.
No, Roger, no, as you came you may go,
 Clumpaty, clumpaty, clump.

Oh! what is the reason, dear Dolly, he cried,
 Pumpaty, pumpaty, pump.
That thus I'm cast off and unkindly deny'd,
 Frumpaty, frumpaty, frump.
Some rival more dear I guess has been here,
 Crumpaty, crumpaty, crump.
Suppose there's been two; pray, sir, what's that to you?
 Numpaty, numpaty, nump.

O, then with a sigh a sad farewell he took,
 Lumpaty, lumpaty, lump.
And all in despair he leapt into the brook,
 Flumpaty, flumpaty, flump.
His courage it cool'd, he found himself fool'd,
 Trumpaty, trumpaty, trump.
He swam to the shore and saw Dolly no more,
 Rumpaty, rumpaty, rump.

And then she recall'd and recall'd him again,
 Humpaty, humpaty, hump.
But he like a madman ran over the plain,
 Stumpaty, stumpaty, stump.
Determin'd to find a damsel more kind,
 Plumpaty, plumpaty, plump.
While Dolly's afraid she shall die an old maid,
 Mumpaty, mumpaty, mump.

HENRY CAREY (1693?-1743)

On the Oldpark Road
WHERE I DID DWELL

On the Oldpark Road, where I did dwell,
Lived a butcher's son, whom I knew so well,
He courted me, till my heart was sore,
Then left me standing at the door.

He took a strange girl on his knee,
And he told her things that he never told me
And now I know the reason why,
Because she had more gold than I.

But her gold will melt,
And his love will die,
And she will be as poor as I.

ANONYMOUS

Belfast street-song

THE THREE DANISH GALLEYS

Three galleys come sailing to Porlock Side,
And stole me away a new-wed bride,
> *Who left my true love lying dead on the shore,*
> *Sailing out and away.*
> *I never shall see my dear home no more.*

Then up to her stepped the Danish King,
And her he would wed with a golden ring,
> *Who left my true love lying dead on the shore,*
> *Sailing out and away.*
> *I never shall see my dear home no more.*

The bride she made answer her tears between,
I never will wed with a cowardly Dene.
> *Who left my true love lying dead on the shore,*
> *Sailing out and away.*
> *I never shall see my dear home no more.*

Then out of the galley they tossed the Bride,
And laughed as she drowned in the cruel tide.
> *Who left my true love lying dead on the shore,*
> *Sailing out and away.*
> *I never shall see my dear home no more.*

There came three small galleys from Porlock Bay,
They fought with the Danes for a night and a day.
> *Who left my true love lying dead on the shore,*
> *Sailing out and away.*
> *I never shall see my dear home no more.*

They fought till the decks with blood ran red,
And every man of the Danes was dead.
> *Who left my true love lying dead on the shore,*
> *Sailing out and away.*
> *I never shall see my dear home no more.*

Then back into Porlock they towed the Bride,
And buried her down below the Tide.
    Who left my true love lying dead on the shore,
    Sailing out and away.
    I never shall see my dear home no more.

ANONYMOUS

Dene: local pronunciation of 'Dane'
This very early ballad probably dates from Anglo-
Saxon times. It was an ancient belief that to bury a
drowned corpse below the tide-line would prevent its
ghost from walking.

YOUNG WATERS

About Yule, when the wind blew cule,
   And the round tables began,
O there is come to our King's court
   Mony a well-favor'd man.

The Queen luikt owre the castle-wa',
   Beheld baith dale and down,
And there she saw Young Waters
   Come riding to the town.

His footmen they did rin before,
   His horsemen rade behind;
Ane mantel of the burning gowd
   Did keip him frae the wind.

Gowden-graith'd his horse before,
   And siller-shod behind;
The horse Young Waters rade upon
   Was fleeter than the wind.

Out then spak' a wylie lord,
   Unto the Queen said he:
'O tell me wha's the fairest face
   Rides in the company?' —

'I've sene lord, and I've sene laird,
   And knights of high degree,
But fairer face than Young Waters'
   Mine eyne did never see.'

Out then spake the jealous King,
   And an angry man was he:
'O if he had bin twice as fair,
   You micht have excepted me.'

'You're neither laird nor lord', she says,
    'But the King that wears the crown;
There is not a knight in fair Scotland
    But to thee maun bow down'.

For a' that she cou'd do or say,
    Appeas'd he wad nae bee,
But for the words which she had said,
    Young Waters he maun dee.

They hae ta'en Young Waters,
    And put fetters to his feet;
They hae ta'en Young Waters, and
    Thrown him in dungeon deep.

'Aft have I ridden thro' Stirling town,
    In the wind but and the weet;
But I neir rade thro' Stirling town,
    Wi' fetters at my feet.

'Aft have I ridden thro' Stirling town,
    In the wind but and the rain;
But I neir rode thro' Stirling town
    Neir to return again'.

They hae ta'en to the heiding-hill
    His young son in his craddle;
And they hae ta'en to the heiding-hill
    His horse but and his saddle.

They hae ta'en to the heiding-hill
    His lady fair to see;
And for the words the Queen had spoke
    Young Waters he did dee.

ANONYMOUS

> *round tables:* meetings of knights and nobles
> arranged by Kings in the age of chivalry
> *gowden-graith'd:* wearing golden harness
> *heiding-hill:* beheading-hill; place of execution

MY FATHER WAS FROM RONDA

My father was from Ronda,
My mother from Antequera;
The Moors took me prisoner
Between peace and war,
And they bore me off to sell me
At Jeréz de la Frontera.
Seven days and their nights
I was there at auction;
Not a Moorish man nor woman
Would give money for me
Except for one dog of a Moor
Who gave a hundred gold pieces,
And to his house took me
And snapped a chain on me
And he gave me a foul life,
A black life he led me:
Pounding hemp by day,
By night milling fodder
With a bit in my mouth
Lest I should eat any,
And my hair in a knot,
And I went round on a chain.
But as pleased God in heaven
He had a kind housekeeper:
When the Moor went hunting
From the chain she released me
And in her lap took me
And picked the lice from my head;
For a favour that I did her
One far greater she did me:
She gave me the hundred gold pieces
And sent me back to my country,
And thus it pleased God in heaven
That I came to safety.

ANONYMOUS

translated from the Spanish by W. S. Merwin

THE HIGHWAYMAN

I am a wild and wicked youth,
I love young women and that's the truth,
I love them dearly, I love them well,
I love them better than tongue can tell.

I never robbed not a poor man yet,
I never caused any tradesman to fret.
I robbed Lord Golding, I do declare,
I left him bleeding in Grosvenor Square.

'Twas about seventeen I took a wife,
I loved her dearly as I loved my life,
And to maintain her both fine and gay
I went a robbing on the highway.

Six pretty maidens shall carry you,
Six pretty maidens shall bury you,
Six pretty maidens shall bear your pall,
Give them white gloves and pink ribbons all.

So it's dig me a grave both large, wide and deep
And a marble stone at my head and feet
And in the centre a turtle dove
To show mankind I died for love.

ANONYMOUS

KING RENAUD

King Renaud from war returned
With his guts into his hand.
His mother from the battlement high
Called to her son where he went by:

'Renaud, Renaud, rejoice and sing,
Your wife is brought to bed of a king.'
'Neither of wife nor of son,' quoth he
'Can I rejoice or merry be.

'Go, mother, go before me,' he said,
'And bid them make up a fair white bed.
Little time shall I lie there:
I die at midnight, upon the hour.

'But let them bring down my cot,
That a woman in labour hear me not.'
And when the hour of midnight tolled,
King Renaud yielded up his soul.

Before the day began to break
The varlets all went for his sake;
It had not come to breakfast-time,
The maidservants wept at his name.

'Tell me, tell me, mother my dear,
Why are the servants weeping here?'
'Daughter, down by the ford they found
The best of all our horses drowned.'

'And why, why, mother my dear,
Weep for a horse so loud and drear?
When King Renaud comes again,
He'll bring better horses home.

'Tell me, tell me, mother my dear,
What is the knocking that I hear?'
'Daughter, I bade carpenters come
To mend the floorboards in that room.'

Now when she rose up from her bed,
And that she would to mass be led
And when a week was past and gone
She wanted to put on her gown.

'Tell me, tell me, mother my dear,
What gown to-day shall I wear?'
'Take the green, take the grey,
Take the black to wear this day.'

'Tell me, tell me, mother mine,
Why should I wear a black gown?'
'Women who get up from childbed
Wear black to be well-suited.'

When she came in the church to stand
She took a candle in her hand;
When she came in the church to kneel
Fresh-dug earth lay at her heel.

'Tell me, tell me, mother my dear,
Why is the earth so fresh in here?'
'Daughter, I cannot lie to you:
Renaud is dead and lies below.'

'Since Renaud is dead, whom I loved best,
Here are the keys of my treasure chest;
Take my rings, take my jewels,
Feed well my son Renaud.

'Open the earth wide gaping
That I may go with Renaud, my King.'
Earth opened, earth gaped wide
And swallowed up King Renaud's bride.

ANONYMOUS
translated from the French by Rayner Heppenstall

70

Young Beichan

Young Beichan, he was a noble lord
    And a peer of high degree;
He hath taken ship at London Town,
    For that Christ's Tomb he would see.

He sailéd west, and he sailéd east
    Till he came to Galilee,
Where he was cast in prison strong
    And handled cruelly.

Now in that prison there grew a tree,
    Was wondrous tall and strong;
He was gyvéd by the middle to't,
    That his life might not be long.

The Turk he had a daughter fair,
    Ne'er fairer did man see,
She's stolen the keys of the prison house door,
    Young Beichan to set free.

'O, gin a lady would borrow me,
    At her stirrup-foot I would run.
Or gin a widow would borrow me,
    I would swear to be her son.

'Or gin a virgin would borrow me,
    I would wed her with a ring,
I'd give her halls, I'd give her bowers,
    I'd love her above all thing.'

O barefoot, barefoot gaed she but,
    And barefoot came she ben,
It was not for want of hosen and shoon,
    But for fear of making din.

And when she saw him, Young Beichán,
   Her heart was wondrous sair:
For the mice but and the bold ratóns
   Had eaten his yellow hair.

She gave him a shaver for his beard,
   A comber for his hair,
Five hundred pound in his pockét:
   To spend and not to spare.

'Go, set your foot on good shipboard,
   And haste to your ain countrie,
And before three years are come and gone
   Well married we shall be.'

He had not been in his ain countrie
   A twelvemonth till an end,
But he must marry an earl's daughtér,
   Or else lose all his land.

'Ochone alas!' says Young Beichán,
   'I know not what to dee:
For I cannot win to Burd Isbel,
   And she cannot come to me.'

O, it fell once about that time,
   Burd Isbel lay asleep;
And up there starts the Billie Blin
   That slept at her bed-feet.

'O waken, waken, Burd Isbél!
   How can ye sleep so sound,
When this is Beichan's wedding day,
   All upon English ground?

'Now do ye to your mother's bower,
   Think neither sin nor shame,
But take ye two of your mother's maries
   To keep ye from all blame.

'Then dress yourself in red scarlett,
    And your maries in dainty green;
And put a girdle about your middle,
    Were fit for any queen.

'Then gang ye down by yon sea-side,
    And down by the sea-strand,
So bonny will the Holland boats
    Come rowing to your hand.

'Then set your milk-white foot aboard
    And cry: "Hail ye, Domine!"
And I shall be the steerer o't
    To row you o'er the sea.'

⋆   ⋆   ⋆

She came full soon to Young Beichan's gate,
    And heard the fiddlers play;
Then well she kenned from all she heard
    It was his wedding day.

She's putten her hand in her pockét,
    And taken out guineas three.
'Hey, take ye that, ye proud portér,
    Bid the bridegroom speak to me!'

O, when that he came up the stair,
    He louted to the knee:
'Won up, won up, ye proud portér,
    And what meaneth this courtesy?'

'O, I have been porter at these gates,
    It's thirty years and three;
But there's a lady at them now:
    Her like I ne'er did see.

'For she is dressed in red scarlett,
    Her maries dressed in green;
And she's a girdle about her middle
    Were fit for any queen.

'On every finger she has a ring,
    And on the mid-finger three;
And there's as much gold about her brow
    Would buy an earldom for me.'

Then up it starts him, Young Beichán,
    And he swears by Our Ladie:
'It can be none but Burd Isbel,
    Come o'er the flood to me!'

O, quickly ran he down the stairs,
    Of fifteen made but three;
He's taken Burd Isbel in his arms
    And kissed her tenderly.

'O, have ye forgotten, Young Beichán,
    The vow you made to me,
When I took you out of the prison strong
    And helped you o'er the sea?

'O, have ye taken another bride,
    And have ye forgotten me,
Though I stole the keys of the prison door,
    And gave you liberty?'

She lookéd over her left shoulder
    To hide the tear in her ee:
'Now fare thee well, dear love,' she says,
    'And I'll think no more on thee.'

'Take home your daughter, madam,' he says,
    'With all my lands for fee;
For I must marry my first true love
    That gave me liberty.'

'Is this a custom of your house,
    Or the fashion of your town:
To marry a maid on a May morning
    And send her back ere noon?'

ANONYMOUS

> *gyved:* shackled, fettered
> *borrow:* bail or deliver from prison
> *but:* outer room of a house
> *ben:* inner room
> *ratons:* rats
> *Burd:* lady
> *Billie Blin:* household hobgoblin
> who usually gives good advice
> *do:* go
> *maries:* ladies
> *louted:* bowed
> *won:* rise

Th' Childer's Holiday

Eh, dear, I'm welly off my chump!
I scrub, an' wesh, an' darn;
Eawr childer han a holiday,
An' th' heawse is like a barn.

Yo talk abeawt a home sweet home!
My peace is flown away;
I have to live i' Bedlam for
A fortnit an' a day.

They're in an' eawt from morn to neet,
I met weel look so seawer;
They're wantin' pennies every day,
An' butties every heawer.

They'n worn my Sunday carpet eawt
Wi' runnin' up an' deawn;
Eawr Polly broke a jug today,
An' Jimmy broke his creawn.

They'n nobbut bin a-whoam a week,
But, bless me, heaw they grow;
An' talk o' childish innocence,
The devil's in 'em o.

They'n smashed a brand new dolly tub,
An' o' my clooas pegs;
They'n rattled th' paint off th' parlour door,
An' th' skin off th' table legs.

They started pooin' th' picters deawn,
One neet when I were eawt,
Eawr Tum geet th' 'Rock of Ages', an'
He gave eawr Joe a clout.

Eawr Bill, who has a biggish meawth –
He's allus in disgrace –
Set off cowfin t'other day,
An' went reet black i' th' face.

He'd swallowed th' babby's dummy-tit
Wi' rawngin' wi eawr Bet;
We'n gan him tons of physic; but
We hanno fun it yet.

Eawr Jack's a plester on his nose,
An' th' beggar looks a treat;
He'd pood his tongue eawt to a lad
Who lives i' Stoney-street.

Eawr Bobby's bin i' bed o day,
Poor lad, he does look hurt.
He went o' bathin' yesterday,
An' some'dy stole his shirt.

They're o so full o dirt an' grime,
I'st never get 'em clen;
I'st ha' to scrape 'em when it's time
To go t'schoo again.

Eawr Tommy says he winno' goo,
That lad's a wary wight.
He's had his thumb i' th' mangle, an'
He swears he conno' write.

I sat me deawn o Wednesday neet,
An' th' parson's wife were theer.
I hope hoo didno yer me swear –
They'd put a pin i' th' cheear.

I'd lock 'em up i' th' schoo for good
If I could ha' my will;
I'd see they had another clause
I' th' Education Bill.

I've clouted 'em an' slapped 'em till
My honds an' arms are sore;
I'st fancy I'm i' Paradise
When th' holidays are o'er.

They're like a lot o lunatics,
They'n getten eawt of hond;
But yet, I wouldno part wi' em
For o there is i' th' lond.

SAM FITTON   (1868-1923)

butties: slices of bread and butter
dolly tub: wash tub in which clothes were
stirred with a wooden appliance called a dolly
rawngin': playing about boisterously
wary wight: clever or rather cunning fellow

JUSTICE AND INJUSTICE

JIM JONES AT BOTANY BAY

O listen for a moment, lads,
   And hear me tell my tale,
How o'er the sea from England's shore
   I was compelled to sail.

The jury says, He's guilty, sir,
   And says the judge, says he,
For life, Jim Jones, I'm sending you
   Across the stormy sea.

And take my tip before you ship
   To join the Iron Gang,
Don't be too gay at Botany Bay,
   Or else you'll surely hang.

Or else you'll hang, he says, says he,
   And after that, Jim Jones,
High up upon the gallows tree
   The crows will peck your bones.

You'll have no chance for mischief then,
   Remember what I say,
They'll flog the poaching out of you
   Out there at Botany Bay.

The winds blew high upon the sea,
   And the pirates came along,
But the soldiers on our convict ship
   Were full five hundred strong.

They opened fire and somehow drove
   That pirate ship away.
I'd rather have joined that pirate ship
   Than come to Botany Bay.

For night and day the irons clang,
　　And like poor galley slaves
We toil and toil, and when we die
　　Must fill dishonoured graves.

But bye and bye I'll break my chains,
　　Into the bush I'll go
And join the brave bushrangers there —
　　Jack Donahoe and Co.

And some black night when everything
　　Is silent in the town
I'll kill the tyrants, one and all,
　　And shoot the floggers down.

I'll give the law a little shock,
　　Remember what I say,
They'll yet regret they sent Jim Jones
　　In chains to Botany Bay.

ANONYMOUS

Jack Donahoe was transported as a convict
from Dublin to Australia in 1823. He became
an escapee or 'bolter', and lived for three years
as a bushranger before being killed in a fight
with the Horse Police in 1830.

SHAMEFUL DEATH

There were four of us about that bed;
    The mass-priest knelt at the side,
I and his mother stood at the head,
    Over his feet lay the bride;
We were quite sure that he was dead,
    Though his eyes were open wide.

He did not die in the night,
    He did not die in the day,
But in the morning twilight
    His spirit pass'd away,
When neither sun nor moon was bright,
    And the trees were merely grey.

He was not slain with the sword,
    Knight's axe, or the knightly spear,
Yet spoke he never a word
    After he came in here;
I cut away the cord
    From the neck of my brother dear.

He did not strike one blow,
    For the recreants came behind,
In a place where the hornbeams grow,
    A path right hard to find,
For the hornbeam boughs swing so,
    That the twilight makes it blind.

They lighted a great torch then,
    When his arms were pinion'd fast,
Sir John the knight of the Fen,
    Sir Guy of the Dolorous Blast,
With knights threescore and ten,
    Hung brave Lord Hugh at last.

I am threescore and ten,
   And my hair is all turn'd grey,
But I met Sir John of the Fen
   Long ago on a summer day,
And am glad to think of the moment when
   I took his life away.

I am threescore and ten,
   And my strength is mostly pass'd,
But long ago I and my men
   When the sky was overcast,
And the smoke roll'd over the reeds of the fen,
   Slew Guy of the Dolorous Blast.

And now, knights all of you,
   I pray you pray for Sir Hugh,
A good knight and a true,
   And for Alice, his wife, pray too.

WILLIAM MORRIS (1834-96)

recreants: cowards

Shooting of His Dear

Come all you young people who handle the gun,
Be aware of those shooting between moon and sun.
I've a story to tell you that's happened of late
Concerning Molly Bander whose beauties were great.

Molly Bander were a-walking and a shower came on.
She stopped under a beech-tree the shower to shun.
Jimmy Randal were a-hunting, he were a-hunting in the dark;
He shot his own true love, and he missed not her heart.

And then he run to her and he found her quite dead,
And in her own bosom finding tears he had shed.
He took his gun in his hand, to his uncle did run,
Saying: Uncle, dear uncle, I've killed Molly Ban;
I shot her and killed her. She was the joy of my life.
I always intended for to make her my wife.

Up stepped his old father with his head all so grey,
Saying: Randal, Jimmy Randal, don't run away.
Stay in your own country till your trial comes on;
You shall not be hanged; I'll spend my whole farm.

On the day of his trial her ghost did appear,
Saying: Randal, Jimmy Randal, Jimmy Randal, go clear.
He spied my apron pinned around me, he killed me for a swan.
He shot me and killed me. My name's Molly Ban.

ANONYMOUS

HOMECOMING

A Breton returns to his birthplace
After having pulled off several fast deals
He walks in front of the factories at Douarnenez
He recognizes nobody
Nobody recognizes him
He is very sad.
He goes into a *crêpe* shop to eat some *crêpes*
But he can't eat any
There's something that keeps him from swallowing
He pays
He goes out
He lights a cigarette
But he can't smoke it.
There's something
Something in his head
Something bad
He gets sadder and sadder
And suddenly he begins to remember:
Somebody told him when he was little
'You'll end up on the scaffold'
And for years
He never dared do anything
Not even cross the street
Not even go to sea
Nothing absolutely nothing.
He remembers.
The one who'd predicted everything was Uncle Grésillard
Uncle Grésillard who brought everybody bad luck
The swine!
And the Breton thinks of his sister
Who works at Vaugirard
Of his brother killed in the War
Thinks of all the things he's seen
All the things he's done.
Sadness grips him
He tries again
To light a cigarette

But he doesn't feel like smoking
So then he decides to go see Uncle Grésillard.
He goes
He opens the door
Uncle doesn't recognize him
But he recognizes him
And he says to him:
'Good morning Uncle Grésillard'
And then he wrings his neck.
And he ends up on the scaffold at Quimper.
After having eaten two dozen *crêpes*
And smoked a cigarette.

JACQUES PRÉVERT (1900-77)

translated from the French by Lawrence Ferlinghetti
crêpe: pancake

THE BALLAD OF POSTMAN WILLIAM L. MOORE FROM BALTIMORE

who marched on his own into the Southern States in 1963.
He protested against the persecution of the negroes.
He was shot after a week.
Three bullets struck his forehead.

SUNDAY
Sunday meant rest for William L. Moore
after a hard week's work.
He was only a postman and pretty poor,
he came from Baltimore.

MONDAY
Monday, one day in Baltimore,
he said to Mrs Moore:
I don't want to be a postman no more,
I'm going down south on a tour.
  BLACK AND WHITE, UNITE! UNITE!
  on a placard he wrote.
  White and black — hold repression back!
  And he set off on his own.

TUESDAY
Tuesday, one day on the railway train,
people asked William L. Moore
what was the sign he was carrying,
and wished him luck for his tour.
  BLACK AND WHITE, UNITE! UNITE!
  stood on his placard...

WEDNESDAY
Wednesday, one day in Alabama,
walking down the main street,
still a long way from Birmingham,
he'd already got aching feet.
        BLACK AND WHITE, UNITE! UNITE!

THURSDAY
Thursday, the day the sheriff stopped him,
said, 'What the hell — you're white!
What business of yours is the niggers, man?
If it's trouble you want — all right!'
        BLACK AND WHITE, UNITE! UNITE!

FRIDAY
Friday, a dog started following him,
became his only friend.
By evening stones were hitting them both,
but they went on to the end.
        BLACK AND WHITE, UNITE! UNITE!

SAT'DAY
Sat'day, that day it was terribly hot,
a white woman came up to the two,
gave him a drink and secretly whispered:
'I think the same as you.'
        BLACK AND WHITE, UNITE! UNITE!

LAST DAY
Sunday, a blue and summer's day,
he lay in the grass so green —
three red carnations blooming blood-red
on his forehead could be seen.
        BLACK AND WHITE, UNITE! UNITE!
        stood on his placard.
        White and black — hold repression back!
        And he died on his own.
        And he won't be alone.

WOLF BIERMANN (b. 1936)
translated from the German by Steve Gooch

91

THE YOUTH AND
THE LEOPARD

These were the words of the beardless youth:
'I crossed the rocky mountain ridges,
I went on a hunt, I set off on
the paths that cross the bare, sharp rocks.
High on the crags I came across
a herd or two of mountain goats.
I fired my gun at a great-horned goat,
the horns crashed down to the river's bank.
I had stumbled on a leopard's lair,
the time was the middle of the night.
The leopard flew out in my path,
he filled my god-given eyes with rage.'

Leopard and youth closed in to fight,
they made the earth beneath them quake,
they sent the boulders tumbling down,
they smashed the forest branches off.
The youth was running short of time,
the hilt of his sword was red with blood,
he puts up his shield but cannot fend
the quick-limbed leopard of the rocks.
Its claws lash out and rip apart
the hem of his armoured coat of mail.
Now the youth laid both his hands
to clutch the crosspiece of his sword.
Slowly his sabre cut into the beast,
the time had come for it to fall.
He hurled the leopard from the rock
and turned the sandy river-banks red.
High on the rocks the youth himself
lay on his side and breathed his last.

Who will tell this to his mother?
Fortune-tellers, soothsayers sit at her door.

'After all, our hunter's arrows
were not used up to no avail.'
His mother was walking to and fro,
weeping had filled her eyes with tears.
'A leopard fell upon my son,
a raging, savage leopard. Now
they have blacked out each other's daylight,
my son with the sword, the beast with his limbs.
The leopard could not have been a coward,
my son did not face a gentle beast.
Each has slaughtered his enemy;
shame on them, for neither lives.'

As she wept, she bound the wounds
the leopard's claws had left on her son.
'Child, you are asleep, not dead,
it's hard work that has worn you out.
How could the wild beast rip apart
the shirt of chain-mail that you wore?
You must have been a match for him,
your arms flagged as you swung your sword.
The leopard would not give you time,
nor did you let him have a chance.
The shield you were clutching in your hand
could now no longer cover you;
nor could the leopard use his limbs,
the sword had shattered his bone in two.
This much, no more, I shall weep for you,
your death is not a cause for tears.
Farewell, the sign of the cross be with you;
for this is the gateway to the grave.
At least I have brought up one real son,
a warrior who fought a savage leopard.'

As she slept, the ghosts appeared
now of the leopard, now of her son.
Now the leopard seemed to rip
the iron bodice off her son;
now it seemed her son was winning,
flinging the leopard head over heels.

And, strange to tell, after such dreams
she would awake with sobs and tears.
At times she would think, 'Who ever heard
of any son whom no mother reared?
Perhaps the leopard's mother too
is, like me, crying day and night.
I shall leave and go to her
and give her comfort in her grief,
so that she tells me all her tales
and I shall tell her of my son,
for she is sorrowing for her son,
killed without pity by the sword.'

ANONYMOUS
translated from the Georgian by Donald Rayfield

THE CONVICT
OF CLONMEL

How hard is my fortune
   And vain my repining;
The strong rope of fate
   For this young neck is twining!
My strength is departed,
   My cheeks sunk and sallow,
While I languish in chains
   In the gaol of Clonmala.

No boy of the village
   Was ever yet milder;
I'd play with a child
   And my sport would be wilder;
I'd dance without tiring
   From morning till even,
And the goal-ball I'd strike
   To the lightning of Heaven.

At my bed-foot decaying
   My hurl-bat is lying;
Through the boys of the village
   My goal-ball is flying;
My horse 'mong the neighbours
   Neglected may fallow,
While I pine in my chains
   In the gaol of Clonmala.

Next Sunday the patron
  At home will be keeping,
And the young active hurlers
  The field will be sweeping;
With the dance of fair maidens
  The evening they'll hallow,
While this heart once so gay
  Shall be cold in Clonmala.

JEREMIAH JOHN CALLANAN
(1795-1829)

> *hurl-bat:* stick used in playing hurling,
> in Ireland a game rather like hockey
> *patron:* from the Irish 'patruin',
> a celebration or party
>
> Clonmala is in County Tipperary

TALES OF NEAR AND FAR

THE LITTLE FAMILY

There was a little family
　Who lived in Bethany;
Two sisters and a brother
　Composed this family.

With praying and with singing,
　Like angels in the sky,
At morning and at evening,
　They raised their voices high.

They lived in peace and pleasure
　Though poor for years and years,
Although they laid up treasure
　Beyond this vale of tears.

Though poor and without money,
　Their kindness made amend;
Their house was always open
　To Jesus and his friend.

And thus they lived so happy,
　So poor, so kind, so good.
Their brother grew afflicted
　And rudely throwed in bed.

Poor Martha and poor Mary,
　They wept aloud and cried;
But still he grew no better,
　But lingered on and died.

The Jews came to the sisters,
　Put Lazreth in the tomb,
And tried for them to comfort,
　And drive away their gloom.

When Jesus heard these tidings,
    Though in a distant land,
How swiftly did he travel
    To join this lonely band!

When Martha saw him coming,
    She met him on his way;
She told him that her brother
    Had died and passed away.

He cheered and he blessed her,
    He told her not to weep,
For in him was the power
    To wake him from his sleep.

When Mary saw him coming,
    She ran and met him too,
And at his feet fell weeping,
    Rehearsed the tale of woe.

When Jesus saw her weeping,
    He fell a-weeping too;
He wept until they showed him
    Where Lazreth was in tomb.

He rolled away the cover,
    He looked upon the grave,
He prayed unto his Father,
    His loving friend to save.

Then Lazreth in full power
    Came from the gloomy mound,
And in full strength and vigor
    He walked upon the ground.

Now if we but love Jesus,
    And do his holy will,
Like Martha and like Mary,
    He'll always use us well.

From death he will redeem us,
  And take us to the skies,
Where we will reign forever,
  Where pleasure never dies.

ANONYMOUS

American version from the South
and Middle West of an English
traditional ballad.

See also *St John's Gospel*, Chapter 11.

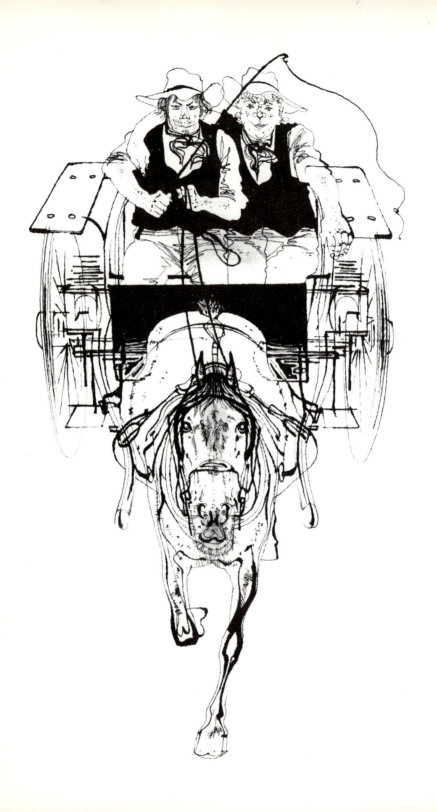

TAVVYSTOCK GOOZEY VAIR

Tes just a month cum Vriday nex' Bill Champernown an' me
Us drov' a crost ole Dartymoor th' Goozey Vair to zee.
Us made oursels quite 'vitty' — us shav'd and grais'd our 'air
An' off us goes in our Zunday cloes be'ind Bill's ole gray mare.
Us smell'd the sage an' onions arl th' way fr'm Whitchurch Down,
An' didn' us av a blawout when us put up in th' town,
An' theer us met Ned 'Annafurd, Jan Steer an' Nicky Square,
Ut sim to we arl Deb'm mus' be to Tavvystock Goozey Vair.
Chorus
An' uts, Aw thun, whur be'e gwaine an' wot be'e doin' of there?
'Aive down yer prong, an' stap down long, tes Tavvystock Goozey
 Vair.

Us went an' zeed th' 'osses, an' th' yaffers, an' th' yaws,
Us went 'pun arl th' round-a-bouts an' inter arl th' shaws
An' then ut started rainin' an' blawin' too, es fai,
So off us goes back to th' 'Rose' an' 'aves a dish o' tay
An' then us 'ad a zing-zong an' th' folks kep' drappin' in,
An' them wot knaw'd us arl cum roun' an' 'ad a drap o' gin
Till wot with one an' t'other us didn' sim to care
Whether us wor to Bellevur Tor er Tavvystock Goozey Vair.
Chorus
An' uts, Aw thun, whur be'e gwaine an' wot be'e doin' of there?
'Aive down yer prong, an' stap down long, tes Tavvystock Goozey
 Vair.

Twus rainin' straims an' dark as pitch when us started 'ome that
 night
An' when us got pas' Merrival Bridge th' mare er tuk a vright.
Says I to Bill, "Be careful er you'll av us in th' drains."
Says Bill ter me, "Be-gad," says 'e, "why, abun' yew got th' reins?"
Just then th' mare run slap agin a whackin' gurt big stoan
'Er kicked th' trap to flibbits and 'er trotted off alone.
When us cum to us reckin'd twarnt no gude settin' there
So us 'ad to trudge 'ome thirteen mile fr'm Tavvystock Goozey
 Vair.

Chorus
An' uts, Aw thun, whur be'e gwaine an' wot be'e doin' of there?
'Aive down yer prong, an' stap down long, tes Tavvystock Goozey
    Vair.

C. JOHN TRYTHALL

vitty: respectable; proper
grais'd: greased, with lard
blawout: a good meal
Deb'm: Devon
whur be'e gwaine: where are you going
stap down long: come (step) along; get moving
yaffers: heifers
yaws: ewes (female sheep)
shaws: side-shows at a fair
es fai: without a shadow of doubt; certainly (perhaps from 'Yes faith' or, even
    earlier, 'Yes by the Fates')
dish o' tay: pot of tea
drains: channel or gutter at the side of the road to carry off water
Merrival Bridge: Merivale Bridge, over the River Walkham on Dartmoor
abun' yew: haven't you
flibbits: pieces; fragments

Tavistock Goose Fair is still held every year on the second Wednesday in
October.

THE ROYAL
FISHERMAN

As I walked out one May morning,
　　When May was all in bloom,
O there I spied a bold fisherman,
　　Come fishing all alone.

I said to this bold fisherman,
　　'How come you fishing here?'
'I'm fishing for your own sweet sake
　　All down the river clear.'

He drove his boat towards the side,
　　Which was his full intent,
Then he laid hold of her lily-white hand
　　And down the stream they went.

Then he pulled off his morning gown
　　And threw it over the sea,
And there she spied three robes of gold
　　All hanging down his knee.

Then on her bended knees she fell:
　　'Pray, sir, pardon me
For calling you a fisherman
　　And a rover down the sea.'

'Rise up, rise up, my pretty fair maid,
　　Don't mention that to me,
For not one word that you have spoke
　　Has the least offended me.

'Then we'll go to my father's hall,
　　And married we shall be,
And you shall have your fisherman
　　To row you on the sea.'

Then they went to his father's house,
  And married now they be;
And now she's got her fisherman
  To row her down the sea.

ANONYMOUS

WILLIE LEONARD, *or*
THE LAKE OF COLD FINN

It was early Monday morning Willie Leonard arose,
And straight to his comrade, young Leonard did go;
Saying, 'Arise, loyal comrade, and let nobody know,
It's a fine summer morning and a-bathing we will go.'

They walked and they talked till they came to a lane,
And the first one they met was a keeper of game;
Saying, 'Go back, Willie Leonard, do not venture in
For there's deep and false water in the Lake of Cold Finn.'

Young Willie stripped off to swim the lake round;
He swam to an island, and came to dry ground,
Saying, 'Comrade, my comrade, don't venture to come in,
For there's depth and false water in the Lake of Cold Finn.'

He went in again to swim it once more;
He swam it most over, but could not find dry shore,
Saying, 'Comrade, loyal comrade, I feel very weak',
And these were the last words Willie Leonard did speak.

It was early next morning Willie's sister arose,
And straight to the bedchamber of her mother she goes;
'Oh, mother, dear mother, I had a strange dream,
I dreamed I saw Willie in a cold watery stream!'

It was early next morning Willie's mother was there,
A-wringing of her hands and a-tearing of her hair;
'Oh, murder, oh, murder, — was there nobody nigh,
That would venture their life for my own darling boy?'

It was early next morning Willie's uncle was there,
And he swam around the lake like a man in despair;
'Was he surely drowned, or did he fall in?
For there's deep and false water in the Lake of Cold Finn!'

The day of Willie's funeral will be a grand sight,
There will be four and twenty young men all dressed up in white;
They will follow his remains till it's laid in the clay,
They will bid young Willie adieu, and they will all march away.

For to see Willie's mother, it would grieve your heart sore,
And to see Willie's sweetheart, it would grieve your heart more,
For every fine morning he would her salute,
With his pinks and red roses and fine garden fruit.

ANONYMOUS

BALLAD BY
HANS BREITMANN

Der noble Ritter Hugo
   Von Schwillensaufenstein,
Rode out mit shpeer and helmet,
   Und he coom to de panks of de Rhine.

Und oop dere rose a meermaid,
   Vot hadn't got nodings on,
Und she say, 'Oh, Ritter Hugo,
   Vhere you goes mit yourself alone?'

And he says, 'I rides in de creenwood,
   Mit helmet und mit shpeer,
Till I cooms into ein Gasthaus,
   Und dere I trinks some beer.'

Und den outshpoke de maiden
   Vot hadn't got nodings on:
'I ton't dink mooch of beoplesh
   Dat goes mit demselfs alone.

'You'd petter coom down in de wasser,
   Vhere dere's heaps of dings to see,
Und hafe a shplendid tinner
   Und drafel along mit me.

'Dere you sees de fisch a schwimmin',
   Und you catches dem efery von:' —
So sang dis wasser maiden
   Vot hadn't got nodings on.

'Dere ish drunks all full mit money
   In ships dat vent down of old;
Und you helpsh yourself, by dunder!
   To shimmerin' crowns of gold.

'Shoost look at dese shpoons und vatches!
  Shoost see dese diamant rings!
Coom down and fill your bockets
  Und I'll giss you like efery dings.

'Vot you vantsh mit your schnapps und lager?
  Coom down into der Rhine!
Der ish pottles der Kaiser Charlemagne
  Vonce filled mit gold-red wine!'

Dat fetched him — he shtood all shpell pound;
  She pooled his coat-tails down,
She drawed him oonder der wasser,
  De maiden mit nodings on.

CHARLES GODFREY LELAND (1824-1903)

St George and the Dragon

Of Hector's deeds did Homer sing;
  And of the sack of stately Troy,
What griefs fair Helena did bring,
  Which was Sir Paris' only joy:
And by my pen I will recite
St George's deeds, an English knight.

Against the Sarazens so rude
  Fought he full long and many a day;
Where many giants he subdu'd
  In honour of the Christian way:
And after many adventures past
To Egypt land he came at last.

Now, as the story plain doth tell,
  Within that country there did rest
A dreadful dragon fierce and fell,
  Whereby they were full sore opprest:
Who by his poisonous breath each day,
Did many of the city slay.

The grief whereof did grow so great
  Throughout the limits of the land,
That they their wise-men did intreat
  To shew their cunning out of hand;
What way they might this fiend destroy,
That did the country thus annoy.

The wise-men all before the king
  This answer fram'd incontinent;
The dragon none to death might bring
  By any means they could invent:
His skin more hard than brass was found,
That sword nor spear could pierce nor wound.

When this the people understood,
　　They cried out most piteously,
The dragon's breath infects their blood,
　　That every day in heaps they die:
Among them such a plague it bred,
The living scarce could bury the dead.

No means there were, as they could hear,
　　For to appease the dragon's rage,
But to present some virgin clear,
　　Whose blood his fury might assuage;
Each day he would a maiden eat,
For to allay his hunger great.

This thing by art the wise-men found,
　　Which truly must observed be;
Wherefore throughout the city round
　　A virgin pure of good degree
Was by the king's commission still
Taken up to serve the dragon's will.

Thus did the dragon every day
　　Untimely crop some virgin flower,
Till all the maids were worn away,
　　And none were left him to devour:
Saving the king's fair daughter bright,
Her father's only heart's delight.

Then came the officers to the king
　　That heavy message to declare,
Which did his heart with sorrow sting;
　　She is, quoth he, my kingdom's heir:
O let us all be poisoned here,
Ere she should die, that is my dear.

Then rose the people presently,
　　And to the king in rage they went;
They said his daughter dear should die,
　　The dragon's fury to prevent:
Our daughters all are dead, quoth they,
And have been made the dragon's prey:

And by their blood we rescued were,
   And thou hast saved thy life thereby;
And now in sooth it is but fair,
   For us thy daughter so should die.
O save my daughter, said the king;
And let *mè* feel the dragon's sting.

Then fell fair Sabra on her knee,
   And to her father dear did say,
O father, strive not thus for me,
   But let me be the dragon's prey;
It may be, for my sake alone
This plague upon the land was thrown.

'Tis better I should die, she said,
   Than all your subjects perish quite;
Perhaps the dragon here was laid,
   For my offence to work his spite:
And after he hath suckt my gore,
Your land shall feel the grief no more.

What hast thou done, my daughter dear,
   For to deserve this heavy scourge?
It is my fault, as may appear,
   Which makes the gods our state to purge;
Then ought I die, to stint the strife,
And to preserve thy happy life.

Like mad-men, all the people cried,
   Thy death to us can do no good;
Our safety only doth abide
   In making her the dragon's food.
Lo! here I am, I come, quoth she,
Therefore do what you will with me.

Nay stay, dear daughter, quoth the queen,
   And as thou art a virgin bright,
That hast for virtue famous been,
   So let me clothe thee all in white.
And crown thy head with flowers sweet,
An ornament for virgins meet.

And when she was attired so,
  According to her mother's mind,
Unto the stake then did she go;
  To which her tender limbs they bind:
And being bound to stake a thrall,
She bade farewell unto them all.

Farewell, my father dear, quoth she,
  And my sweet mother meek and mild;
Take you no thought nor weep for me,
  For you may have another child:
Since for my country's good I die,
Death I receive most willingly.

The king and queen and all their train
  With weeping eyes went then their way,
And let their daughter there remain,
  To be the hungry dragon's prey:
But as she did there weeping lie,
Behold St George came riding by.

And seeing there a lady bright
  So rudely tied unto a stake,
As well became a valiant knight,
  He straight to her his way did take:
Tell me, sweet maiden, then quoth he,
What caitiff thus abuseth thee?

And lo! by Christ his cross I vow,
  Which here is figured on my breast,
I will revenge it on his brow,
  And break my lance upon his chest:
And speaking thus whereas he stood,
The dragon issued from the wood.

The lady that did first espy
  The dreadful dragon coming so,
Unto St George aloud did cry,
  And willèd him away to go;
Here comes that cursed fiend, quoth she,
That soon will make an end of me.

St George then looking round about,
    The fiery dragon soon espy'd,
And like a knight of courage stout,
    Against him did most fiercely ride;
And with such blows he did him greet,
He fell beneath his horse's feet.

For with his lance that was so strong,
    As he came gaping in his face,
In at his mouth he thrust along;
    For he could pierce no other place:
And thus within the lady's view
This mighty dragon straight he slew.

The savour of his poisoned breath
    Could do this holy knight no harm:
Thus he the lady sav'd from death,
    And home he led her by the arm:
Which when King Ptolemy did see,
There was great mirth and melody.

When as that valiant champion there
    Had slain the dragon in the field,
To court he brought the lady fair,
    Which to their hearts much joy did yield.
He in the court of Egypt stayed
Till he most falsely was betray'd.

That lady dearly lov'd the knight
    He counted her his only joy;
But when their love was brought to light,
    It turn'd unto their great annoy:
Th' Morocco king was in the court,
Who to the orchard did resort,

Daily to take the pleasant air,
    For pleasure sake he us'd to walk,
Under a wall he oft did hear
    St George with Lady Sabra talk:
Their love he shew'd unto the king,
Which to St George great woe did bring.

Those kings together did devise
    To make the Christian knight away,
With letters him in courteous wise
    They straightway sent to Persia:
But wrote to the Sophy him to kill,
And treacherously his blood to spill.

Thus they for good did him reward
    With evil, and most subtilly
By such vile means they had regard
    To work his death most cruelly;
Who, as through Persia land he rode,
With zeal destroy'd each idol god.

For which offence he straight was thrown
    Into a dungeon dark and deep;
Where, when he thought his wrongs upon,
    He bitterly did wail and weep:
Yet like a knight of courage stout,
At length his way he digged out.

Three grooms of the King of Persia
    By night this valiant champion slew,
Though he had fasted many a day;
    And then away from thence he flew
On the best steed the Sophy had;
Which when he knew he was full mad.

Towards Christendom he made his flight,
    But met a giant by the way,
With whom in combat he did fight
    Most valiantly a summer's day:
Who yet, for all his bats of steel,
Was forc'd the sting of death to feel.

Back o'er the seas with many bands
    Of warlike soldiers soon he passed,
Vowing upon those heathen lands
    To work revenge; which at the last,
Ere thrice three years were gone and spent,
He wrought unto his heart's content.

Save only Egypt land he spar'd
  For Sabra bright her only sake,
And, ere for her he had regard,
  He meant a trial kind to make:
Meanwhile the king, o'ercome in field,
Unto Saint George did quickly yield.

Then straight Morocco's king he slew,
  And took fair Sabra to his wife,
But meant to try if she were true
  Ere with her he would lead his life:
And, tho' he had her in his train,
She did a virgin pure remain.

Toward England then that lovely dame
  The brave St George conducted strait,
An eunuch also with them came,
  Who did upon the lady wait;
These three from Egypt went alone.
Now mark St George's valour shown.

When as they in a forest were,
  The lady did desire to rest;
Meanwhile St George to kill a deer,
  For their repast did think it best:
Leaving her with the eunuch there,
Whilst he did go to kill the deer.

But, lo! all in his absence came
  Two hungry lions fierce and fell,
And tore the eunuch on the same
  In pieces small, the truth to tell;
Down by the lady then they laid,
Whereby they shew'd, she was a maid.

But when he came from hunting back,
  And did behold this heavy chance,
Then for his lovely virgin's sake
  His courage strait he did advance,
And came into the lions' sight,
Who ran at him with all their might.

117

Their rage did him no whit dismay,
   Who, like a stout and valiant knight,
Did both the hungry lions slay
   Within the Lady Sabra's sight:
Who all this while sad and demure,
There stood most like a virgin pure.

Now when St George did surely know
   This lady was a virgin true,
His heart was glad, that erst was woe,
   And all his love did soon renew:
He set her on a palfrey steed,
And towards England came with speed.

Where being in short space arriv'd
   Unto his native dwelling place;
Therein with his dear love he liv'd,
   And fortune did his nuptials grace:
They many years of joy did see,
And led their lives at Coventry.

ANONYMOUS

Sophy: the ruler of Persia

DUKE WILLIAM'S FROLIC

Duke William and a Nobleman, heroes of England's nation,
One morning, nigh to two o'clock did take their recreation;
Into the country they did go, in Sailors' dress from top to toe,
Said Duke William, now let us go and know, how they use the
   brave Sailors.

Dress'd all in their sailor's trim, they straightway hastened to an
   inn,
And when they were there, they made all the people stare at their
   manly appearance,
The landlady viewed them; by good words they assail her,
Said she, come in, be not afraid, I love the jolly sailor.

Then upstairs they did go, and in a room did enter,
The Duke did say, landlady, please bring wine both white and
   red,
Before the wine was drunk out, a press gang bold and stout,
In the lower rooms for sailors bold did look and search about.

The landlady said, go upstairs, if sailors you are seeking,
But one's so fat that I believe you'll hardly care to ship him;
Ne'er mind, the press gang they did say, and went without delay,
We're jolly sailors, brothers, from what ship are you, we pray?

We do belong to George, said Will; said they, where's your
   protection?
We've none at all, they did reply, don't cast on us reflection:
The lieutenant then did say, brothers, come without delay,
They shall not make you a prey, our warrant is for Sailors.

They led them to their leader then, the Captain did them meet,
The Duke, he said, kind gentlemen, take great care of your sheep;
With that, the Captain, he did swear, I am your shepherd, I
   declare,
We'll make you know you saucy are, get down among the sailors.

The Nobleman he did go down, but the Duke he refused,
At which the officers did frown, and sadly him abused;
Where must I lie? his highness said, may I not have a feather bed?
You're fat enough, they all replied, pig in amongst the sailors.

Then straight below the Duke did go, unto his comrade, Sir,
How he did swear to see the fate of many a brisk young blade, Sir,
Below, he tore his trousers, and, calling for some tailors,
The Captain said, you saucy blade, there's no one here but sailors.

For your bold airs, the Captain said, you'll surely get a flog, Sir,
Quick to the gangway him convey, and whip him like a dog, Sir,
Come strip, he cried; the Duke replied, I do not like your law, Sir,
I ne'er will strip for to be whipped, so strip me if you dare, Sir.

Then instantly the Boatswain's mate began for to undress him,
But presently he did espy the star upon his breast, Sir,
Then on their knees they straight did fall, and for mercy soon did
   call,
He replied, you're base villains, thus using us poor Sailors.

No wonder that my royal father cannot man his shipping,
'Tis by using them so barbarously, and always them a whipping,
But, for the future, sailors all, shall have good usage, great and
   small,
To hear the news, together all cried, may God bless Duke William.

He ordered them fresh officers that stood in need of wealth,
And with the crew he left some gold, that they might drink his
   health,
And when that they did go away, the sailors loud huzzaed,
Crying, blessed be that happy day whereon was born Duke
   William.

ANONYMOUS

The ballad tells of a supposed early adventure of the third son of George III,
who was created Duke of Clarence in 1789. He later became William IV
(1765-1837) and was known as the 'Sailor King.'

THE BOLD DRAGOON, *or*
THE PLAIN OF BADAJOS 1812

'Twas a Maréchal of France, and he fain
  would honour gain,
And he long'd to take a passing glance at
  Portugal from Spain;
    With his flying guns this gallant gay,
    And boasted corps d'armée −
O he fear'd not our dragoons, with their
  long swords, boldly riding,
    Whack, fal de ral, &c.

To Campo Mayor come, he had quietly
  sat down,
Just a fricassee to pick, while his soldiers
  sack'd the town,
    When, 'twas peste! morbleu! mon General,
    Hear the English bugle-call!
And behold the light dragoons, with their
  long swords, boldly riding,
    Whack, fal de ral, &c.

Right about went horse and foot, artillery
  and all,
And, as the devil leaves a house, they
  tumbled through the wall;
    They took no time to seek the door,
    But, best foot set before −
O they ran from our dragoons, with their
  long swords, boldly riding,
    Whack, fal de ral, &c.

Those valiant men of France they had
  scarcely fled a mile,
When on their flank there sous'd at once
  The British rank and file;
    For Long, De Grey, and Otway, then
    Ne'er minded one to ten,
But came on like light dragoons, with their
  long swords, boldly riding,
    Whack, fal de ral, &c.

Three hundred British lads they made
  three thousand reel,
Their hearts were made of English oak,
  their swords of Sheffield steel,
    Their horses were in Yorkshire bred,
    And Beresford them led;
So huzza for brave dragoons, with their
  long swords, boldly riding,
    Whack, fal de ral, &c.

Then here's a health to Wellington, to
  Beresford, to Long,
And a single word of Bonaparte before I
  close my song:
    The eagles that to fight he brings
    Should serve his men with wings,
When they meet the bold dragoons, with their
  long swords, boldly riding,
    Whack, fal de ral, &c.

SIR WALTER SCOTT (1771-1832)

sous'd: pounced upon

JOHN GRIMALDI, *or*
THE SAILOR'S RETURN

Not all forgotten yet in London Town
Is Joe Grimaldi, once the famous Clown.
Though vanished from the Stage these many moons
Men know what songs he sang, if not the tunes.
Some hint or shadow of his figure lingers
In ancient prints of pits and clowns and singers.
And many know he played the tragic part
Of making merry with a broken heart.

Who was this darling of that distant age?
An actor's son, born almost on the stage.
Theatre-drawn with every breath he drew.
(He played a monkey's part ere he was two).
He, and his younger brother John, were both
Theatre-doomed, Joe willingly, John loth.
Birth-doomed, to drag through childhood's bitter days
On scanty bread from tiny parts in plays,
Joe, glad, however bitter it might be,
John, loathing all, and longing for the sea.

John, being seven, brighter hopes began;
A berth was found him in an Indiaman,
His kit was given and aboard he went,
Bound for the Spice Isles of the Orient
Or so he hoped, but found a long delay
Of toil in port ere getting under way.
Toil all unwelcome to a tiny boy
Expecting liberty and sailor's joy
And finding thraldom and unwelcome cheer
Salt, dark and dirty in a cable-tier
With none to teach him, save by kick and blow,
The unknown art he was supposed to know.

There, as he sorrowed, sailor-sick and sad,
Another prospect opened to the lad.
A near-by frigate had command to sail
Next day at dawn should wind and tide avail.
Surely, in her, he would at once achieve
The grand, free life of men who cannot grieve,
Who sail upon white wings as Neptune's sons
Annihilating England's foes with guns;

Then, rich with prize, return in glory, singing,
Setting the Minster bells of England ringing...
Surely, in her...
               Thus little boys of seven
Dream of the life at sea as life in Heaven.
So, in the dusk, this little John, stripped bare
And left his Indiaman at anchor there,
And swam, all naked, to the frigate's side,
To volunteer where no-one was denied.
But to what tests they put him, and what rank
He climbed to in that peril of sea-plank,
Is all unknown, his person disappears,
No word of him is heard for fourteen years.

Meanwhile his brother Joe, by slow degrees
Learned upon jealous stages how to please,
Learned all the craft, and met with John again,
While playing comedy in Drury Lane.
While in the wings and waiting for his cue
A man said, 'Joe, some people ask for you.
Two men: they wait below, till you are free.'

Thither Joe went; gay sprigs they seemed to be,
Elegant youths, and strangers both, he thought.
But one most pressingly his notice caught,
Showing a tiny scar upon his chest,
It was John's self, his brother manifest,
Returned, and rich, for as he made avow,
'I have six hundred pounds upon me now.'
'John there is danger laying such facts bare.'
'Sailors despise all danger everywhere.'
'In town, they should not; but, I must not stay.

Come to the Green Room till we end the play.
Wroughton is there, who fitted you for sea.'

Then John's companion uttered hastily,
'I'll call for you tomorrow, John, at ten.'
This John confirmed, the friend departed then.
It was remembered later, none had heard
Aught of this friend, no name, nor other word,
Nor noticed him, save that, like John, he bore
Gear ready-made, as one just come ashore.
Blue coat, white waistcoat, and a gold-topped cane,
Thus geared, he left and never came again.

Within the Green Room, John made many friends,
Joe came and went at scene and curtain ends;
But when the play was over Joe was free.
'John, when I've changed, you must come home with me.'
And here he told of Mother, Wife and home,
And what a joy it was that John had come,
To share their life: and asked, How long ago
John had reached town.
                        'Two hours' time, or so...
Time just to dine and come to Drury Lane.'
'When I have changed I'll take you home again.'
And here he named the number and the street.
'Now I will change: wait here until we meet.'

Leaving John there, Joe hurried off to change.
But John's arrival had made all seem strange,
All marvellous, miraculous, undreamed...
Changing his clothes took longer than he deemed.
But having dressed, an actor hailed him thus:
'Ah, Joe, what fun for you and all of us...
Your brother's on the stage, that lively blade...
He says you've been much longer than you said.'

John was not on the stage; a man said, 'No...
I saw him here not twenty ticks ago...
He went towards the stage-door, down the stair.'
Joe hurried thither, but John was not there.
'Went out a minute since,' the porter cried,

'No, not so much: he must be just outside...'
But no John showed in the dim lamp-lit lane,
No John at all was there, so much was plain.
'Of course', Joe cried, 'there where the windows glow...
The Bowlbys live: he knew them long ago.
Young Bowlby was his friend: he's calling there.'
Thither they went, but found the covert bare.
'Yes. John was here not half a minute past!'
Old Bowlby said, 'That's where I saw him last
Going to Duke Street, just beyond the bend.'
'Baily's,' said Joe, 'our landlord, then, and friend.
He's gone to Baily's. On, to Baily's all.'

Blank windows watched the night from Baily's wall...
Joe knocked and rang: but nobody replied.
At last an upper window opened wide.
A maid put head out, 'As I said before...
He's not at home...stop knocking at the door.'
       'Who's not at home?'
            'Why, Mr Baily, sir.'

Within the darkened house, there came a stir,
A light, the maid descended, and unchained.
'A man came knocking here, Sir,' she explained.
'Rousing the street, Sir, not a minute past.
Our Mr Baily left here Friday last...
Going to Hungerford, out Berkshire way...
I told the man, Sir, and he went away.
And when you knocked, I thought he'd come again.
From up above I could not see him plain.
Only his waistcoat white...'

          'Well...it was John.
He came to look-up Baily and has gone...
Gone to the theatre, no doubt, for me.

       Back to the theatre, then, hurriedly.'
Joe thanked the girl, and hurriedly returned.

The theatre was shut, though light still burned,
Men, closing-down, unbolted to the knock.
No-one had entered since they turned the lock,

John was not there, had never come again.
'He has gone home to Mother, it is plain.'
Joe said, 'I told him the address; he's there.'
So, swiftly, by still street and empty square,
By cats and watchman's braziers, and odd light,
Late cart or passer, of a town at night,
He hurried home, and knocked, and was let in.

Strangeness had shewn; now tragedies begin.
Joe found his Mother pale, and asked in doubt,
'Has anybody called, since I went out?'
'No-one...Who should have called?'
         'Your son, John, home.'
The Mother swooned; alas, no John had come,
And though she hoped the night through, did not com

But John's companion (Joe remembered, then)
Had clearly said, 'I'll call for you at ten.'
So, before ten, Joe was on watch again
In and about the doors of Drury Lane
But neither John nor friend th' appointment kept.

Joe and his Mother waited, watched and wept.
Asked, sought, entreated, but they never heard
Of brother John again one helpful word.

No littlest trace of him was ever found.
By many means Death brings us to the ground,
But where or by what means Joe's brother died
None came to know, though many seekers tried.
The tiny glimpse of one who knocked by night
Caught by the maid, the half-seen glimpse of white,
Remained the last glimpse seen of brother John.
From darkness come and into darkness gone.

Some thought a press-gang hurried him aboard
A ship at point to sail to death abroad.
Some, that a tempter lured him into hold
Near Drury Lane, and killed him for his gold.
Some, that the unknown friend had plotted this.
Cities and Night hide many mysteries.

Some have imagined that he came to knock
His Mother's door and begged her to unlock.
Calling himself, 'Your John, returned from sea'...
That she refused, a lone, weak woman she...
There, in an unlit suburb, late at night...
That, then, at her refusal, in despite,
He had abandoned every thought of home,
And turned to that unknown whence he had come.

Some ask, if that that Drury Lane perceived
Were, truly, living man, as men believed,
Not ghost or phantom of John newly dead
Fulfilling hope long unaccomplishéd,
Through thwarting Death upon fulfilment's brink?
Longing for home is stronger than men think
And after fourteen years of sea, at war,
Starved of all tenderness men hunger for,
The longing may have focused to such flame
That it out-struggled Death and overcame
Allowing the loosed soul to have her will.

So some have wondered, as they wonder still.
The answer to the problem no man knows.
The hearts that ached have finished now with woes.

JOHN MASEFIELD (1878-1967)

The actor Joseph Grimaldi (1779-1837) first
appeared on the stage as an infant dancer at Sadler's
Wells in 1781, and at Drury Lane took part in his
first pantomime either in that same year or the year
following. As a clown, he is said never to have had an
equal.

SONG

King Julius left the south country
His banners all bravely flying;
His followers went out with Jubilee
But they shall return with sighing.

Loud arose the triumphal hymn
The drums were loudly rolling,
Yet you might have heard in distance dim
How a passing bell was tolling.

The sword so bright from battles won
With unseen rust is fretting,
The evening comes before the noon,
The scarce risen sun is setting.

While princes hang upon his breath
And nations round are fearing,
Close by his side a daggered death
With sheathless point stands sneering.

That death he took a certain aim,
For Death is stony-hearted
And in the zenith of his fame
Both power and life departed.

EMILY BRONTË (1818-48)

Julius is invading and claiming the throne
of Gondal, an imaginary kingdom
invented by the sisters Emily and Anne
Brontë and about which they made up
many stories in tiny handwritten booklets.
The texts of these tales have never been found.

Acknowledgments

Michael Baldwin, *Dunkley's Dewpond,* from HOB AND OTHER POEMS. Reprinted by permission of Michael Baldwin and Chatto & Windus, Ltd.

Wolf Biermann, *The Ballad of Postman William L. Moore from Baltimore* (translated from German by Steve Gooch), from POEMS AND BALLADS by Wolf Biermann. Reprinted by permission of Pluto Press Ltd. Translation copyright © Steve Gooch 1977.

Ed. Keith Bosley, the anonymous poem *The Youth and the Leopard* (translated from Georgian by Donald Rayfield) from THE ELEK BOOK OF ORIENTAL VERSE, 1979. Reprinted by permission of Paul Elek Ltd.

Robert Graves, *Goliath and David,* from GEORGIAN POETRY, ed. James Reeves. Reprinted by permission of Robert Graves.

Christopher Hampton, *Origin of Fire,* from SAVAGES by Christopher Hampton. Reprinted by permission of Faber and Faber Ltd.

John Harris, *The Burial,* from SONGS FROM THE EARTH: SELECTED POEMS OF JOHN HARRIS, CORNISH MINER, 1820-1884, ed. D. M. Thomas (The Lodenek Press).

Rayner Heppenstall, *King Renaud,* from THE INTELLECTUAL PART by Rayner Heppenstall. Reprinted by permission of Rayner Heppenstall.

Ted Hughes, *The Golden Boy,* from SEASON SONGS by Ted Hughes. Reprinted by permission of Faber and Faber Ltd.

Jan Kasprowicz, *The Day before Harvest* (translated from Polish by Jerzy Peterkiewicz and Burns Singer), from FIVE CENTURIES OF POLISH POETRY. Reprinted by permission of Anthony Sheil Associates Ltd.

Philip Larkin, *The Explosion,* from HIGH WINDOWS. Reprinted by permission of Faber and Faber Ltd.

Ed. MacEdward Leach, the anonymous poems *Willie Leonard, or the Lake of Cold Finn* and *The Little Family,* from THE BALLAD BOOK, ed. MacEdward Leach. Reprinted by permission of A. S. Barnes & Company, Inc.

John Masefield, *John Grimaldi,* from THE BLUEBELLS by John Masefield. Reprinted by permission of The Society of Authors as the literary representative of the Estate of John Masefield.

Ed. W. S. Merwin, the anonymous poem *My Father was from Ronda* (translated from Spanish by W. S. Merwin). Reprinted by permission of Abelard-Schuman Limited.

Ed. Colette O'Hare, *On the Oldpark Road, where I did dwell,* from WHAT DO YOU FEED YOUR DONKEY ON?, ed. Colette O'Hare (Collins Publishers).

Brian Patten, *The Mule Laden with Corn, The Mule Laden with Gold,* from THE SLY CORMORANT AND THE FISHES by Brian Patten. Reprinted by permission of Penguin Books Ltd. Copyright © 1977 by Brian Patten.

Jacques Prévert, *Homecoming* (translated from French by Lawrence Ferlinghetti), from SELECTIONS FROM PAROLES by Jacques Prévert. Reprinted by permission of City Light Books. Copyright © 1947 by Editions du Point du Jour.

C. John Trythall, *Tavvystock Goozey Vair.* Reprinted by permission of Edwin

Ashdown Ltd.

W. B. Yeats, *The Ballad of Moll Magee,* from COLLECTED POEMS. Reprinted by permission of M. B. Yeats and the Macmillan Co. of London & Basingstoke.

INDEX OF POETS